Lisa Costello

Native Indian/Neo American

Lisa Costello

Native Indian/Neo American

Examining the Conflicting Elements of Leslie Marmon Silko's Work and their Influence on her Literary Career

VDM Verlag Dr. Müller

Impressum/Imprint (nur für Deutschland/ only for Germany)
Bibliografische Information der Deutschen Nationalbibliothek: Die Deutsche Nationalbibliothek verzeichnet diese Publikation in der Deutschen Nationalbibliografie; detaillierte bibliografische Daten sind im Internet über http://dnb.d-nb.de abrufbar.

Coverbild: www.purestockx.com

Verlag: VDM Verlag Dr. Müller Aktiengesellschaft & Co. KG
Dudweiler Landstr. 99, 66123 Saarbrücken, Deutschland
Telefon +49 681 9100-698, Telefax +49 681 9100-988, Email: info@vdm-verlag.de

Herstellung in Deutschland:
Schaltungsdienst Lange o.H.G., Berlin
Books on Demand GmbH, Norderstedt
Reha GmbH, Saarbrücken
Amazon Distribution GmbH, Leipzig
ISBN: 978-3-639-11604-5

Imprint (only for USA, GB)
Bibliographic information published by the Deutsche Nationalbibliothek: The Deutsche Nationalbibliothek lists this publication in the Deutsche Nationalbibliografie; detailed bibliographic data are available in the Internet at http://dnb.d-nb.de.

Cover image: www.purestockx.com

Publisher:
VDM Verlag Dr. Müller Aktiengesellschaft & Co. KG
Dudweiler Landstr. 99, 66123 Saarbrücken, Germany
Phone +49 681 9100-698, Fax +49 681 9100-988, Email: info@vdm-verlag.de

Printed in the U.S.A.
Printed in the U.K. by (see last page)
ISBN: 978-3-639-11604-5

To Mam
For all your love, support and guidance

CONTENTS

INTRODUCTION	**Background & Early works**	**1 - 9**
CHAPTER 1	**Ceremony**	**10- 23**
CHAPTER 2	**Almanac of the Dead & Map**	**24 – 35**
CONCLUSION	**Gardens of the Dunes**	**36 – 40**
WORKS CITED		**41 -42**
WORKS CONSULTED		**43**

Acknowledgements

Special thanks must be given to Dr Lee Jenkins whose contribution was absolutely invaluable. I am immensely grateful for her continuous support and guidance. I am also grateful to Dr Padraig Kirwan of the University of London, whose enthusiasm for the subject was a constant motivation. I would like to thank my family and my friends who are my reason for living and for laughing. Anne, thanks for all the motivating phone calls and Gill, thanks for the laughter, the stress and most importantly, the Java.

Introduction

Since its recognition as a distinct genre, Native American Literature has been shrouded in controversy. Although writings by so called natives have been in evidence since the late nineteenth century, the academic field of Native American Literature is a relatively new area of interest. In 1969 academics specialising in the genre were almost non existent. Writings by American Indians were rarely included in university courses and social barriers prevented them from being taught in schools. However civil rights and feminist movements of the 1980s, along with specific texts such as N Scott Momadays House made of Dawn and Vine Deloria's Custer died for your Sins removed the majority of these social barriers giving the field of Native American Literature the freedom to mature. As the genre developed, critics and professionals encountered a new problem; that of defining its parameters. The question "What is Native American Literature?" still causes much controversy within the academic community. Many academics refuse to consider written works as Native American since the Indian culture is an oral one. According to them "Literature ceases to be Indian when it employs Western forms such as the short story or novel"(Weaver, 47). The intermarriage of Natives with white settlers has produced generations of authors who are mixed blood and so this contributes to the problem of characterising the genre for as Thomas King states "Perhaps our simple definition that Native American Literature is literature produced by Natives will suffice for the while providing we resist the temptation of trying to define a native"(Weaver 47). The one element which seems to unite writers of this genre is an acknowledgment of the influence that history has had on their writing. It is impossible to fully comprehend the genre of Native American Literature and the burdens which its author's carry without an awareness of the country's traumatic past.

The history of the American Indian has been a history of genocide from the time that Christopher Columbus first opened the way for European exploration, exploitation and colonisation of the continent of America. When he arrived in the new world Columbus found that the natives did not speak his language and so he deemed them to have no language of their own. He mistakenly called these people *Indios*- Indians because he believed he had landed on islands off the coast of Asia. The natives primitive traits convinced Columbus of their inferiority and he determined that they should be "made to work, sow and do all that is necessary and to *adopt our* ways" (qtd in Brown, 1). Although Columbus's attitude appears to have been that of the benevolent father, in actuality the phrase "adopt our ways" marked the beginning of centuries of oppression and degradation for the Indian people.

This belief in the inferiority of the natives was widely held by the European nations that followed Columbus to the New World. Believing that it was their God given right to explore and conquer, Spain, France and England battled each other for centuries to gain complete control of this new land. Conquering nations would settle for nothing less than the total subjugation of the various tribes they encountered. Modern records show that colonising nations took control of over 95% of Indian lands due to a programme of "discovery" which displaced the Indians as original inhabitants of the continent. The effect of colonisation on the native Indian population was devastating. Between 1500 and 1900 almost sixty million Indians died as a result of contact with white settlers. Disease was the biggest threat to native populations with records showing that 70%-90% of the original Indian population died during first contact. Smallpox, measles and pneumonia were some of the unfamiliar diseases which killed millions. Tribes who attempted to retain hold over their land or natural resources were dispatched in the most brutal manner. Intertribal warfare allowed individual tribes to be subdued or slaughtered one by one by the white invaders who used this division among the natives to their advantage. Goods imported by the white colonists, such as alcohol, did untold damage to the native populations and the fur trade which was introduced by the French created a cycle of violence, dependency and poverty. The settlers also brought a new religion and attempted to convert the indigenous population, mostly by force.

Many tribes attempted to prevent the occupation of their lands by demonstrating their willingness to help in times of war. During the American War of Independence, many Indian tribes fought on the side of the British since their lands were threatened by expanding American settlement. However this war proved to be "an unmitigated catastrophe of incalculable proportion"(Page 226) for the natives. They were portrayed by the victorious nation as bloodthirsty savages whose violence was uncontrollable. The Indians' part in the war sealed their fate, as the United States, citing American right of conquest, forcibly settled Indian lands.

By the 1880s virtually all tribes of the west and some of the east were banished to reservations located far from their ancestral lands. The Indian Removal Act which was passed in 1830 legitimised the federal appropriation of Indian lands and the exile of all Indians west of the Mississippi river. This Act was devastating to a people whose entire way of life was connected to the earth on which they lived. Severed from the land which they had inhabited for thousands of years, Indian tribes were relocated to government reservations. The land on these reservations was poor and did not provide adequate food. Indians were forced to depend on government rations which often did not arrive or if

they did were rotten and inedible. Forbidden to hunt and without proper clothing or housing, many Indians simply died of starvation and exposure. Some tribes imitated the white way of life in the hope that they would be allowed to remain on their tribal lands. The Cherokee tribe embraced this white way of life wholeheartedly establishing a national council and police force and even owning slaves.
They contested the Indian Removal Act and the Supreme Court ruled in their favour. However this decision was overruled by President Andrew Jackson and the Cherokee were forced to migrate in the harshest winter conditions. One in four of the tribe died on the journey known as the *Trail of Tears*.

Some Indian tribes of the Southwest were allowed to remain on part of their ancestral lands. The Navajo were given 3.5million acres in the late nineteenth century and managed to acquire more by simply occupying vacant land and exercising squatters' rights.

The Pueblo Indians who occupied the high desert plateaus of the Southwest remained for the most part on their ancestral lands. However since these lands were colonised by the Spanish, the natives were forced to adapt their ways to accommodate foreign traditions. By the 1900s violent outbreaks by Indians were at an all time low with most tribes living on reservations, totally dependent on the government for food and clothing. As Jake Page states in his book In the Hands of the Great Spirit:

> By the beginning of the Twentieth Century it was perfectly clear that any future for the Indian people in the United States rested almost entirely in the hands of the federal government, even though that government was still relentlessly pressing for the allotment in severalty of Indian lands and the sale of the excess to non Indians- all this under the flag of assimilation, meaning in effect *no separate future* (336).

Having relocated the majority of Indians west of the Mississippi the US government then set about attacking Indian tribalism. Indian children were forcibly taken from their homes and sent to be educated at boarding schools. This was, as David Adams claims, an "education for extinction" (qtd in Porter & Roemer, 52). The aim was to alienate the children from the tribal way of life, effectively leading to its destruction. Students were forbidden from speaking their native languages. They were forced to "learn the practical arts and the mechanical arts, and being away from home often for years at a time, they would *not* learn from uncles and aunts and other elders the old stories of tribal origins, and old morality tales, and other pieces of mythological wisdom"(Page 310). During the summer holidays students were placed with white families who often treated them as servants. Years spent in white schools led to the alienation of Indian children from their culture, but neither were they fully integrated into white society. As a result, generations of Indians were born who occupied a place between the two, part of both worlds but belonging to neither: a part and apart.

In 1924 that the Indian Citizenship Act was passed, granting full citizenship to all Indians living in the United States. Prior to this they had been classified as resident aliens.

The passing of this Act marked an awakening of Indian consciousness which hailed the opening of a new era. Both politically and culturally the Indian people became more active on the American scene. Books written by Indian authors became popular. The origins of Native American Literature can be traced to the 17th century where missionaries began to compose religious texts in the Massachusetts language. However actual publications by natives did not materialize until the late 18th century when protestant missionaries swept across America as part of the religious movement known as the Great Awakening. These missionaries taught the Indian how to read and write English as part of their process of civilisation. From the beginning, this genre of literature has been utilised to highlight the injustices Indian people suffered at the hands of their European colonisers. One of the first autobiographical Indian novels entitled A Son of the Forest was written by William Apess in 1829. This novel dealt with the evils of alcohol and its effects on the native population as it described the abuse William suffered at the hands of his alcoholic grandparents.

By the early1930s literature was emerging as a strong new vehicle for Indian oral traditions. Indian novelists wrote about the colonisation of their lands and the resulting conflict between economic progress and their traditional way of life. As the 20th century progressed Native American Literature broadened its context inducing much critical debate over its position and purpose within the world of literature. Critics such as Geary Hobson have suggested that through literature Indians have discovered a means of preserving their heritage:"By making literature, like the singers and storytellers of earlier times, we serve the people as well as ourselves in an abiding sense of remembrance"(Weaver 52). Professionals such as Gerald Vizenor believe that native literature has, and should continue to be, used as a weapon of resistance against European invasion: "The postindian warriors encounter their enemies with the same courage in literature as their ancestors once envinced on horses and they create their stories with a new sense of survivance"(Weaver 53). Other critics have embraced the notion that Native American writers feel a deep sense of obligation towards their communities and that therefore they write with a "consciousness of responsibility as a member of a living Native American culture"(Weaver 51). Writers such as Simon Ortiz, N Scott Momaday, Vine Deloria and Elizabeth

Cook- Lynn have used literature as a tool to highlight issues of Indian concern and express a shared consciousness.

Although she is frequently classified as a Native American author, Leslie Marmon Silko's work defies such a simplistic definition. She refuses to be restricted to the traditional characteristics of minority writing and continues to push boundaries and conquer the preconceptions of the modern world. Described by critics as Indian, feminist, literary art or political commentary, her work crosses boundaries which have been in place for centuries. Her work provides a bridge between the world of the traditional and the contemporary. Because of her ability to embody these dualistic tensions in her work Silko has been hailed as one of the most important Native American Writers of her generation.

Born in Albuquerque, New Mexico in 1948, Silko was raised on the Laguna Pueblo reservation in northern New Mexico. The environment created by surrounding family members proved to be a great influence on both her early life and literary career. From its beginnings Silko's family has demonstrated a merging of Anglo and Laguna culture. Her great grandfather Robert and his brother were white men who worked on the reservation as surveyors in the 1880s. These men married Laguna women and settled on the reservation. Both were integrated into the community and each in their turn served as mayor of the Pueblo. After the death of his first wife, Robert married her younger sister, Silko's great grandmother, Marie Anaya Marmon. In her youth Marie had attended the Carlisle Indian School in Pennsylvania and wrote and spoke English very well. She was an accomplished storyteller and spent time with the children, especially Silko, telling them traditional Laguna stories but also reading to them from the Bible. Of all her family, Silko was most influenced by this woman, lovingly called "Grandma A'Mooh". She represents the dualistic nature of many Indians at that time, having been born a Laguna Indian but raised in the white education system.

Silko's great aunt Susie was also an important influence on Silko's early life. Having been sent away to school Susie turned her white education into something that could sustain her people, writing down the tribal myths while also developing a reputation as a skilled storyteller within the tribe.

According to Pueblo culture the spoken word was sacred and the storyteller occupied a place of vital importance in the tribe. Faced with the problem of encroaching technological societies, storytelling allowed the pueblo people to retain their identity. Not only were stories a means of entertainment, they were in essence tribal autobiographies; a way to record and pass on the history of the tribe while also demonstrating moral values. According to Carol Mitchell stories are "the heritage of a people; they validate the traditions of a culture, they make the past come alive in the present, and they reassure that the past will continue into the future" (Mitchell 28).

Robert Nelson argues that the actual location of the Marmon house within the Pueblo also accounts for the dual influence of Anglo and Indian on Silko in her early life. The house and the general store which her father ran were located near a major highway bringing the family into contact, not only with Indians from other Pueblos, but also a steady stream of truckers and automobilists. Born and raised at this cultural intersection, Silko was subjected to both modern Anglo and Laguna cultural traditions. During her early life she spent much of her time outdoors, riding off to explore the hills which surround the Pueblo. These solitary rides instilled in Silko a great love of the land and a kinship with her surroundings which comes through vividly in her writing:

> I was never afraid or lonely though I was high in the hills, many miles from home...because I carried with me the feeling id acquired from listening to the old stories, that the land all around me was teeming with creatures that were related to human beings and to me"(qtd in Thompson, 155)

Having attended the Bureau of Indian Affairs school until fifth grade, Silko then moved to parochial schools in Albuquerque before attending the University of New Mexico.

After receiving an honours degree in English she then enrolled in the American Indian Law Program at the University of New Mexico law school. Law was a popular choice of study among young Indians who hoped that an insight into the legal system would aid them in their fight for justice. Silko was no different. However she quickly became disillusioned with the law and transferred to the creative writing programme in the same university. Here Silko found the political forum which she so desperately sought. In her upbringing she was exposed to the traditional and the contemporary in equal measure and as a result speaks out of a mixed blood consciousness. Because of her mixed heritage Silko views herself as something of an outsider and through her writing she attempts to reconcile both her Indian and her European blood: "At the core of my writing is the attempt to identify what it is to be a half breed or mixed blood person, what it is to grow up neither white nor fully traditional Indian" (qtd in Weaver 76)). She vividly recalls days in her youth when the children of the Pueblo would be asked to pose for photographs taken by white visitors. She was frequently excluded from these pictures because her appearance was not considered Indian enough for the tourists. Incidents such as this illustrate Silko's confusion with her identity. Standing waiting to be photographed by white people for money was degrading and yet she felt unhappy to be excluded from this shame because it set her apart from the other children. However instead of rejecting her mixed blood status, Silko has embraced the dual sensibility and utilised it to great effect in her work.

Silko's cultural background and education have created a hybrid author, one with loyalties to both the traditions of her Laguna family and to the contemporary society in which she was educated. In contrast to other Native American authors such as N Scott Momaday and James Welch, who write solely from an Indian perspective, Silko has chosen to embrace her twofold heritage. In her work she examines and expresses the duality which has affected every aspect of her life. Describing her heritage in an interview, Silko stated "At the core of my writing is the attempt to identify what it is to be a half breed or mixed blood person, what it is to grow up neither fully white nor fully traditional Indian" (qtd. In Weaver 22). This message is stressed strongly in much of Silko's work. She has chosen to embrace that element which separates her from her peers. Her early writing is dominated by the expression of ethnic identity and the conflicts it creates when combined with contemporary ideals. Her first published short story, 'The Man to send Rain Clouds' depicts the confusion inherent in the merging of the traditional with the contemporary. When an old Indian man dies his grandchildren send for the local priest to sprinkle water on his grave, not to save his immortal soul as the priest believes, but so that he will not be thirsty in the afterlife. This simple story illustrates at the most basic level the conflicts which arise from the merging of two cultures so wholly different from each other. This issue of conflicting cultures is developed in her best known novel Ceremony.

Chapter One

The novel Ceremony is an important illustration of the issues which permeate every facet of Silko's work. The double consciousness of traditional Indian and contemporary American is strongly illustrated in this work. The novel is based on what has been termed "the reluctant return of the native" (qtd in Clements 68) theme which portrays the return of a main protagonist, Tayo to his reservation after having fought the Japanese in World War 11. The character of Tayo himself represents the double consciousness examined in Silko's work. His very blood is a mixture of these two cultures and as a result of this Tayo inhabits the periphery of both worlds living within the confines of both but fully accepted by neither. When his drunken mother is finally unable to care for him, Tayo is sent to live with his aunt's family on an Indian reservation. A constant reminder of his mother's shame, he is never fully accepted into his aunt's family. During his childhood this distance between Tayo and his Indian relatives is maintained by his aunt who refuses to allow her own son to refer to Tayo as brother and excludes him from family activities.

Tayo's female relatives also reflect the dual influence of Indian and white culture. However the ties to their ethnic identity are much stronger than Tayo's. Both his Aunt Thelma and his mother Laura are, to varying degrees, influenced by the Anglo society which encroaches on their tribal life. Laura is a perfect illustration of the drastic effect which white education had on the mindset of younger Indians. She is taught at school to be ashamed of her own culture and to emulate the styles of dress and modes of behavior of white people-"She looked at her own reflection in windows of houses as she passed; her dress, her lipstick, her hair-all was done perfectly, the way the home ec teacher taught them, exactly like the white girls" (68-69).

Flattered by the attention she receives from the white men, Laura is lured into a life of depravity, violence and alcohol. Although she quickly realises the true nature of her situation, she is unable to break free from the vicious cycle in which she is trapped:

> She was excited to see that despite the fact that she was an Indian, the white men smiled at her from their cars as she walked from the bus stop...but after she had been with them, she could feel the truth in their fists and in their greedy feeble lovemaking; but it was a truth which she had no English words for (69)

Unable to face this truth Laura leaves the reservation in search of acceptance from this white culture which she so desperately longs to call her own. While living on the streets of a nearby city she descends further into a life of prostitution and alcohol, eventually abandoning her son.

In traditional tribal life, one's identity was connected to the community. The tribe was perceived as one complete unit, instead of multiple individuals. Traditionally this was necessary for survival as a distinct group was stronger than several people alone. In this way one single person represented the entire tribe. As a result the loss of one girl to the encroaching alien culture affects her entire tribe. To the old Indians Laura represents what is happening to their culture as a whole-"The people wanted [Laura] back. Her older sister must bring her back. For the people it was that simple, and when they failed, the humiliation fell on all of them; what happened to the girl did not happen to her alone, it happened to all of them"(69). Thelma is given the responsibility, by the elders of the village, for saving her younger sister from her depraved life and returning her to the safety of her people. When Laura gives birth to a child by a white man, Thelma has no choice but to raise him as her own, because Indian rules of lineal descent dictate that the child is now hers. Although Thelma accepts the boy into her home, she does not treat him with kindness. Instead she visits a kind of mental torture on him, doting on her own son while constantly excluding him.

This treatment of Tayo is a conscious action on Thelma's part as, when the rest of the family is present, she treats him as she does her own son. To her, the boy is a living representation of her sister's shame and so through her treatment of him she is venting her anger at her sister's betrayal of their people.

Thelma has also inherited from her people a keen understanding of the old ways but conflicting with this is the encroaching white religion which "separated the people from themselves"(68). A fear of being trapped "in one of the oldest ways"(67), her own Indian mindset, leads Thelma to embrace the white man's religion with its doctrine of guilt, shame and forbearance. Adherence to this religion gives her a superiority over her family and, as she believes, a standing in the community-"Tayo wondered if she liked it that way, going to church by herself, where she could show the people that she was a devout Christian and not immoral or pagan like the rest of the family"(77). Thelma also believes in the superiority of the white way and encourages her son to embrace its teachings-"She wanted him [Rocky] to be a success. She could see what white people wanted in an Indian, and she believed this way was his only chance" (51). Rocky's death in the war and Tayo's subsequent illness simply feeds into Thelma's Christian doctrine of sufferance and forbearance. She feels that she can now hold her head high in the community because her son gave his life and her nephew his sanity in service to the white world. However she is confounded in her support of the outside culture by her mother. In Ceremony, Grandma exemplifies all that is traditional, staunchly adhering to the ancient beliefs. As Edith Swan states, she "embodies the traditional Laguna ethos in counterpoint to the bicultural entrapment in which

Auntie struggles" (313). When modern medicine is unsuccessful in curing Tayo, Grandma calls in the village medicine man, Ku'oosh. However when traditional Indian medicine is also proven ineffective she insists that Tayo visit Betonie, an Indian healer who has embraced new healing practices. Although she is old and blind this woman exudes a strength and wisdom which clearly signifies her as head of the family. A skilled storyteller, she represents one of the most powerful figures in Native American society. Traditionally the strength of a tribe lay in its ability to operate as a community and at the heart of that community was the storyteller. This person occupied a place of importance and strength within the tribe. In Indian culture the stories and myth are "the heritage of a people; they validate the traditions of the culture, they make the past come alive in the present, and they reassure that the past will continue into the future"(Mitchell, 28). As a storyteller, Grandma attempts to educate her grandchildren in the old ways with these "time immemorial" stories. However she not only tells stories for entertainment or for moral instruction but through them passes on the tribe's history to the next generation. Unlike Auntie, whose existence is ruled by village gossip, Grandma is unconcerned what stories the people spread about her family because "If she had a better one about them, then it didn't matter what they said"(89). As head of the family it is fitting that Grandma is the last character to speak in the novel. Her parting remark illustrates the Indian belief that time is cyclical, not linear- "It seems like I already heard these stories before… only thing is, the names sound different"(260). Grandma adheres to the traditional belief that all things which have happened will occur again and the purpose of this is for people to learn so that mistakes will not be repeated. Grandma's last words are also a demonstration of native storytelling techniques, signifying the end of the story and the return to "reality". Through the use of traditional techniques Silko is not only illustrating the native belief in the cyclical nature of life, but also ending her novel on a traditional note, once again aligning herself with her Indian heritage.

To most Indians on the reservation Tayo is a symbol of the corruption of Indian culture: a reminder that both the old ways and the younger generation are being lost to an encroaching Euramerican culture. When he returns from the war, Tayo is lost and confused about his place within the Indian society in which he has been raised. Unable to overcome his illness, he has lost the connection to the people and traditions which surround him.

His experience of white education has also alienated him from the Indian way of life. He is taught in school that the practices of the old people on the reservation are superstitious nonsense. Informed by a white teacher that flies are dirty creatures and carry disease, Tayo is confused when his uncle Josiah informs him that, according to legend the green bottle fly saved their people from death, and so should be respected. Conflicting views such as these lead Tayo to examine the nature of the society in which he lives:

> In school the science teacher had explained what superstition was, and then held the science textbook up for the class to see the true source of explanations. He had studied those books, and he had no reason to believe the stories any more. The science books explained the causes and effects. But old Grandma always used to say, "Back in time immemorial, things were different, the animals could talk to human beings and many magical things still happened." He never lost the feeling he had in his chest when she spoke those words, as she did each time she told them stories; and he still felt it was true, despite all they had taught him in school (95)

The conflict which Tayo's confusion represents was a real problem for Indian children who attended white schools and was encountered by Silko herself. By ridiculing the beliefs of the natives white educators succeeded in alienating the younger generations from the beliefs of their ancestors, casting them adrift in a sea of uncertainty and confusion. When Tayo returns from the war this is the situation he is faced with. Detached from his fellow Indians and from the natural world around him he is unable to comprehend and deal with his wartime experiences. His treatment at the white hospital not only proves futile but actual hinders his recovery. The white doctors attempt to dismiss his sickness as battle fatigue and treat him accordingly. This has no effect whatsoever and leaves Tayo confined to a bed vomiting almost incessantly. Unable to understand the nature of his sickness the doctors send him back to the reservation.

When Tayo's grandmother calls in a traditional medicine man to cure him, Tayo recognises almost immediately that this man will be as ineffectual as the white doctors. Ku'oosh attempts to heal Tayo in the traditional manner, the way it has been done for centuries. However he does not fully understand the cause of the young man's illness. When Tayo confesses that he is unsure if he killed any of the enemy Ku'oosh is confused:

> In the old way of warfare, you couldn't kill another human being in battle without knowing it, without seeing the result, because even a wounded deer that got up and ran again left great clots of lung blood or spilled guts on the ground…But the old man would not have believed white Warfare- killing across great distances without knowing who or how many had died. It was all too Alien to comprehend (36)

Ku'oosh's knowledge of healing is connected to the traditional and so he is unable to comprehend and therefore heal Tayo's illness. Through this character Silko makes the statement that "slavish adherence to static traditional forms is just as unproductive for Native Americans as total assimilation into Euro-American culture" (Clements 72).

In a final act of desperation Tayo is sent to an unconventional healer who lives in the hills outside the town of Gallup. Like Tayo, this character represents a combination of both Indian and white culture. An Indian of mixed blood, Betonie succeeds in helping Tayo because he embraces new practices and recognises the need for change- "At one time, the ceremonies s they had been performed were enough for the way the world was then. But after the white people came, elements in this world began to shift; and it became necessary to create new ceremonies" (126). The old ceremonies could not help Tayo because they were stagnant, never altering over the centuries. Betonie comes from a line of medicine men and women who began to slightly alter the ceremonies to meet the changes occurring in the world around them.

His grandmother tells him "things which don't shift and grow are dead things" (126). Although the people are wary of Betonie and want to believe he is just a crazy old man, they continue to consult him for cures because his ceremonies have been successful. Regarded as something of a renegade, Betonie lives alone in a hogan overlooking the town of Gallup. It seems a strange place for a medicine man to live but, as he tells Tayo, his family occupied their piece of land first and the town simply grew up around them. Instead of moving off to a more isolated spot the medicine man's family uses the town to their advantage, observing the people and the new problems they face and so have proved more effective in their cures than the traditional medicine men who live on the reservations. Betonie was also sent away to school by his grandmother to learn the English language and has taken train rides all over America to collect telephone books and calendars because he likes "keeping track of things" (121). According to David Rice, Betonie has "collected his experience and knowledge to help Indians recognise themselves within the contemporary world and integrate it as part of their experience without letting it overtake them" (126). The information gathered has kept Betonie up to date on modern development and thus he is more qualified to treat Tayo than either Ku'oosh or the white doctors.

Betonie's social marginalization gives him an overview of both Indian and White cultures and he attempts to share this with Tayo. He sees links and bridges between the two cultures that the Indians on the reservation cannot because they are blinded by the traditions of their culture. When Tayo explains how, in the jungle, he confused a Japanese soldier with his uncle Josiah, Betonie replies "It isn't

surprising you saw him with them. You saw who they were. Thirty thousand years ago they were not strangers. You saw what the evil had done: you saw the witchery ranging wide as this world" (124). What Indians call 'white witchery', Betonie attributes to a greater force which attempts to corrupt Indians and whites alike so that they will destroy each other-"That is the trickery of the witchcraft...They want us to believe all evil resides with white people.
Then we will look no further to see what is really happening". This is similar to what Tayo feels even though he is not sure of it himself. He himself sees his sickness as part of something larger. The ceremony that Betonie performs for him is an amalgamation of traditional and modern elements and it helps Tayo in his process of recovery. However, as Silko herself states it is not the ritual itself which heals Tayo but what she calls a *greater Ceremony* – "Tayo's healing is connected to the faith which this old medicine man had, a faith which went back to things far in the past, the belief that its human beings, not particular races or cultures, which will determine whether the human race survives" (Arnold, 35). By reminding Tayo of his humanity, Betonie gives him the strength to resist the illness and heal himself.

The cattle which Josiah purchases are an important element in the story of Tayo's recovery. These beasts are different from the cattle traditionally raised on the reservations. They are hardy and have a strong sense of survival. They are the "descendants of generations of desert cattle, born in dry sand and scrubby mesquite" (74). Josiah intends to replace his old stock which cannot survive the droughts with this new hardy breed. These cattle are a symbol of Tayo and his Indian peers who must adapt if they are to survive. If they do not they will lose their connection to the land and therefore their culture. They will become scared and lost and as Josiah emphatically declares "scared animals die off easily" (74).

The character of Betonie advocates this change which Josiah recognises is necessary. In his conversations with Tayo he encourages the Indian people to stop using the past as a means to escape the present; to stop blaming the white people for all their misfortune and accept some responsibility for their own actions. Betonie recognises that the Indian's anger and resentment and fear of the loss of their culture are preventing progress. Through this character Silko attests that Native American culture can survive if it is flexible enough to accommodate change. Betonie is a mixture of the old and new, performing the old ceremonies but in a new way.
According to Rice, the healer's ceremonies "challenge EurAmerican stereotypes of Native American ritual as codified and stagnant and thus unable to survive the change of EurAmerican encroachment and expansion" (127). Through this character Silko is attesting that it is possible to change to adapt to

the new world while also retaining knowledge of their customs and a link to their heritage. She encourages the Indian people to recognise their brutal history, but not to let the knowledge destroy them.

This message that change is needed for progression is a central theme in Silko's work. Her very career as a writer advocates this. Traditionally Indian culture is oral, with stories and myths being passed on from generation to generation by word of mouth. Silko herself admits that "Among the Pueblo people, a written speech or statement is highly suspect because the true feelings of the speaker remain hidden as he reads words that are detached from the occasion and the audience"(qtd in Brown, 173). Like Betonie, Silko is continuing an ancient custom, that of passing on stories to the next generation, but she is doing it through the modern medium of the written word. As David Beidler states "Silko's work is a study in cultural mediation and spirit[ual] transformation" (1). The very structure of the novel reflects this duality of the traditional and the contemporary. According to Carol Mitchell, the book itself is a curing ceremony-"it weaves the old stories and traditions into the contemporary story of Tayo in a way that helps to make the old ways understandable and relevant to the contemporary situation" (28). Silko uses both prose and poetic forms to tell the story of Tayo, a half breed Indian whose experiences in World War II have damaged him, in both body and mind. The prose section of the novel provides the events of Tayo's life, his childhood, his experiences in the war and his sickness after he returns. However alongside this story Silko has set a series of traditional myths, legends and tribal stories of the pueblo and Navajo people. These various pieces of poetry, story and song form the backbone of the novel, providing a moral backdrop against which the modern story is set. The opening story acts as a framing device for the novel as a whole. It tells the story of Ts'its'tsi'nako, thought woman, an ancient Indian figure who has the ability to make what she thinks actually happen. Silko introduces the prose section, Tayo's story, with the phrase "Im telling you the story/ She is thinking" (1). This technique of distancing the story about to be told from reality is a common device used in the Keres oral tradition. The traditional phrase used to signify the beginning of a story is *humma-hah* which means long ago. This expression is the equivalent of the *once upon a time* framing device used in white culture and declares to the listener, or in this case the reader, that the teller is switching from real time to storytelling time. In using this traditional technique to open her novel, Silko aligns the narrative voice with the Keresan oral tradition and thus lays claim to her Indian heritage. As a result, the structure, as well as the content of the novel depicts the hybridisation which Silko herself represents.

Tayo's need to reconcile his Indian and white blood is the focal point of the novel. At the opening of the story he is lost, cut off from his family, his community and his culture. This according to Silko is devastating for a human being as in Indian society a person's sense of identity is rooted in the community. During his time at the white hospital Tayo refers to himself as white smoke or an invisible thing- "For a long time he had been white smoke…white smoke had no consciousness of itself. It faded into the white world of their bed sheets and walls" (14). Unable to establish a sense of identity Tayo takes on the characteristics of the white world around him. His cousin Rocky is also a deracinated character. Young, ambitious, and intelligent Rocky represents the effect which white education had on generations of Indian children. He is taught at school that the only thing holding him back from a life of success and prosperity in the modern world is the "people at home". As a result he cuts himself off from everything which represents the old ways. In this endeavour he is supported by his mother whose greatest wish is that he "not only make sense of the outside world but become part of it" (76).
And so while Tayo and Josiah are looking after cattle and working all day in the field, Rocky reads magazines and trains for his football scholarship. He is embarrassed by the ancient hunting customs, belittles the views of his elders and constantly tries to cure his grandmother of her 'superstitions'. When his uncle Josiah expresses a view that a book on cattle rearing is of no use because the white author has no idea of the climate in which they raise animals, Rocky replies "Those books are written by scientists. They know everything there is to know about beef cattle. That's the trouble with the way people around here have always done things- they never knew what they were doing"(76). His constant assertion that the modern white way is superior to the traditional means there is no place for Rocky in an Indian world. This is signified by his death in the white man's war. He remains forever caught between a culture which he rejected and one which would not completely accept him.

The conflict between the traditional and the contemporary is also embodied by the characters Harley, Leroy Pinkie and Emo. Their time in the war has made them aware of the contrast between what is Indian and what is white. When these young men joined the army they were treated equally to white soldiers and enjoyed all privileges of the uniform. However when the war was over they were expected to return to their homes and to accept renewed second class citizenship. Unable to readjust to reservation life their existence becomes aimless. They spend days driving around wasting their money in bars, getting drunk and reliving their glorious war days. Tayo alone seems to have understood their position in the white world. He realises that the Indians only use to the white culture was as hired soldiers and sees the irony in the stories told by his friends- "they tried to sink the loss in booze, and silence their grief with war stories about their courage, defending the land they had already lost" (169).

In the case of the character Emo this sense of loss and injustice has a dangerous and violent aspect. Emo represents the inhumanity of the world against which Tayo battles. He is not terrorised by his experiences in the war but embraces the violence, bragging about the prisoners he tortured and the teeth he extracted to keep as souvenirs. His sense of injustice constantly turns to violence which he turns against the white man, Tayo and Harley in turn. Emo represents the greater evil force to which Betonie refers. He constantly reminds his friends of the injustices visited upon their race by the white man and attempts to incite them to violence because "they've [white men] got *everything*. And we don't have shit" (55). Emo allows this knowledge to corrupt him and it causes him to commit murder and forces him to flee the reservation. When Tayo learns of Emo's fate and his supposed destination (California) he muses that the white world is a good place for him. He has been cast out into the white world which he despises so much.

The rift between the Indian people and their culture is evidenced by their alienation from nature and from the animal world, vital elements of Indian heritage. When questioned about the loss of a sheepdog and a flock of sheep Harley replies "They weren't worth anything anyway" (23). This seemingly careless comment is actually a sign of something much bigger. Harley remark represents the white world which sees living things in terms of their monetary value. He has lost his connection to the natural world around him, as have the Indians who live on the outskirts of Gallup. These Indians left the reservation in search of work and a better life than the old people could provide. However exploited and abused by the white world they end up living rough on the streets of city's, too ashamed to return to their people. Overwhelmed by a sense of disconnection and loss these Indians have abandoned their heritage in favor of a white culture that will never accept them. According to Rice, they "are haunted by the fact that their experience in the war has displaced the ethical and historical grounding of native tradition" (116). Their move away from Indian tradition is signified by a move away from the reservation to nearby towns where they try to integrate themselves into white culture. Unfortunately the city provides no refuge for these Indians as yet again they are exploited by white society. Tayo encounters some of these Indians when he visits the healer Betonie in Gallup.

Given only the most menial jobs the reservation Indians are the first to be laid off because "white people in Gallup knew they wouldn't ask any questions or get angry; they just walked away"(115). And so most end up living rough on the streets of the white man's city. By the time these people realise their mistake in leaving the reservation they are too ashamed or too deeply immersed in the white culture to escape. In this way Silko uses the geography of the novel to illustrate the struggle between white and Indian identity. The rural landscape represents the tranquility and simplicity of Indian life. The connection between the sacred and the rural is also stressed. The surrounding desert and mountains would be considered by the modern world as dangerous and threatening places. In Ceremony they are portrayed as places of refuge and security. The final stage of Tayo's healing ceremony takes place on Mount Taylor, or Tse'pina, a mountain considered sacred by the native people. It is there that he meets the character of Ts'eh who represents all that is traditional. She aids Tayo in his recovery by helping him re-establish a connection to the natural world and so to his culture. Tayo also finds a safe haven on the mountain slopes when pursued by the white doctors and police. To these men of the modern world Tse'pina is a dangerous place but for the natives it provides sanctuary. Tayo also experiences his ultimate moment of peace in the rural landscape of the desert which he finally identifies as home

> At that moment in the sunrise, it was all so beautiful, everything, from all directions, evenly, perfectly, balancing day with night, summer months with winter. The valley was enclosing this totality, like the mind holding all thoughts together in a single moment. The strength came from from this feeling. It had always been here. He stood there with the sun on his face, and he thought maybe he might make it after all (237).

In contrast, the urban landscape of the town of Gallup represents the corruption of a white society which views Indians as subservient and yet requires their presence to promote the tourist industry. Indicating the shanty town which his hogan overlooks, Betonie tells Tayo "this is where Gallup keeps Indians until ceremonial time. Then they want to show us off to the tourists". Silko presents the city as violent, noisy and lawless: a desolate place for Indians. It provides nothing in the way of meaningful sustenance. Far from satisfying their religious needs the city does not even meet the Indians material requirements of food and shelter. This is in direct contrast to the rural landscape of the novel which meets both physical and spiritual needs. Also, the Indians in the city occupy a subservient role and are continually exploited by white society. However, although the city represents a negative aspect of white society, it also fulfills an important role in Silko's work-"The place of the city in Silko's cultural dynamic is crucial; urbanisation represents an essential element of Euramerican destructiveness and a necessary aspect of Native American syncreticism and growth" (Rice 115). The corruption of the urban environment is developed further by Silko in her novel Almanac of the Dead which is recognised as her most political work to date.

Chapter Two: Almanac of the Dead

In Almanac of the Dead Silko re-examines and expands the ideas proposed in previous works such as Ceremony. However, where Ceremony is concerned primarily with the plight of an individual, Almanac is more global in its focus. In this novel Silko is repositioning her work in a larger sociopolitical context. She herself stated that "art is the most effective political statement I could make" because "it is more effective to write a story… than to rant and rave" (Arnold 63). This statement echoes the native belief that stories have purpose and power. Traditionally they were told as means of preserving identity but Silko uses her work as a weapon of native resistance. Greeted with a mixture of enthusiasm and criticism by the academic world, Almanac is certainly Silko's most political work to date and has been widely acknowledged as an attack on western culture and capitalism. The novel details five hundred years of oppression and violence, culminating in an era entitled *The Reign of Death Eye Dog*. According to Silko this time will be characterised by excessive brutality and depravity but she also asserts that through revolution redemption is possible. According to Janet St Clair, Silko's focus of attack in Almanac is "explicitly the misogynistic, arrogantly hierarchical, and egocentric traditions of western liberal individualism (141). Corruption in the novel is largely attributed to the rich who are greatly influenced by western, and therefore white, society. As a result the poorer classes (Mexicans, Indians and blacks), are contaminated by their association with this white culture. The novel's timeline spans five hundred years and its content is both historical and prophetic. Critics have claimed that Almanac is the fulfillment of all that Ceremony proposes. Where Ceremony warns that changes are required for the survival of the Indian race, Almanac actually fictionalises these changes. Silko prophesies a cross cultural uprising of oppressed people as the ultimate solution for the survival of all minority cultures.

Throughout the novel various characters are linked through a larger spiritual structure which combats the materialism of contemporary society. These people are seen as a natural force acting as a catalyst for social change. As Romero states "By reconciling ancient prophecy with issues crucial to contemporary American Indian politics, Silko attempts to inspire her readers to resist injustice and secure sovereignty for American Indian peoples and nations through cross cultural coalitions of indigenous peoples dedicated to reclaiming their land"(638).

Set in and around the city of Tucson, Almanac of the Dead depicts a society so corrupt that it is destroying itself from within. The white witchery alluded to in Ceremony by the medicine man Betonie is revealed in all its horrifying clarity. Control seems to be in the hands of the corrupt, as drug addicts and gun smugglers, baby killers and perverts hold key positions of power. Almanac also depicts the corruption of the American legal system through its judge, police and government characters. As stated by St Clair, "In a commodified and atomised society where malevolence and depravity are prerequisites to power and status, the highest and noblest social institutions are inevitable as corrupt as the men who control them"(145). The violence in Almanac is shocking in its extremity as Silko presents the reader with a drastic interpretation of the fate of contemporary society. Although the material content could not be more different from Ceremony, there are tenuous links between the two novels. However Almanac is regarded as a more drastic response by Silko to the injustices suffered by minority cultures under western rule.

In this novel we can again observe the dualistic tensions inherent in Silko's work. As with Ceremony the very structure of the novel illustrates the double consciousness of its author. The book opens with a contemporary framing device in the form of a table of contents and a map which illustrates the history of the Americas for the past five hundred years. Throughout history the map has been regarded as a symbol of the civilised world.

However for many indigenous cultures it has been viewed as a demonstration of colonising force. Silko's map is markedly different from those of contemporary society (See Map at end of Chapter). Instead of geographic locations, it contains a list of the characters in the novel along with the location of ancient monuments significant to native culture. Each of the four corners includes a dialog box which provides not only facts and information on the history of the Americas but also revolutionary messages which proclaim continued "defiance and resistance" to outside threats and prophetic declarations which foretell "The disappearance of all things European". The drawing itself significantly lacks geographical boundaries, containing just one single borderline between the United States and Mexico. However Silko immediately destabilises this border by depicting the mass movement of drugs and guns across it. The map also lacks the linear progression which characterises contemporary maps, instead illustrating circular conceptions of time. As previously discussed in Ceremony the Indian people believed that time was cyclical, and so events taking place have already occurred and will do so again. By taking a symbol of modern culture and using it as a revolutionary tool Silko "critiques official history for its attempts to erase indigenous peoples entirely from the land and history of the southwest" (Romero 630). In using contemporary framing devices to illustrate traditional history, Silko is once again illustrating the hybridity which characterises her work.

The structure of the novel itself also represents the double consciousness of its author. The book addresses modern issues such as drug addiction, gun smuggling and corporate corruption. However these contemporary issues are set within a Native American framework. Stories within stories and characters that are linked in obscure ways give the book a web-like structure, characteristic of the native oral tradition, illustrating circular rather than linear progression. When the character of Sterling, an old Indian, tells his life story he starts, not at the beginning as contemporary society would expect, but halfway through, relating how he arrived at the ranch where he now works.

As the novel progresses fragments of Sterling's life are revealed until we have a complete picture of the character. This somewhat confusion form is repeated throughout the novel. Individual stories are interrupted by tangents which in turn become stories themselves so that the concept of time is confused, focusing our attention on the events themselves, rather than the timeline in which they occur. The content of the novel itself also illustrates the dual influence of Indian and contemporary culture on its author. Modern issues of drug smuggling and police corruption are intertwined with the history of an ancient almanac, and its survival in the modern world. The almanac represents the survival of a people and has been handed down through the generations to two sisters, Lecha and Zeta, who are charged with protecting and transcribing it. However these two sisters are ill equipped to guard such a book. Both women were raised in and greatly influenced by white culture. Lecha has inherited the power to locate and communicate with dead people. However instead of putting her talent to good use she becomes a TV psychic so that she can make money to pay for her drug addiction. Her sister Zeta has stronger ties to her Indian heritage. She alone has inherited the ability to talk to snakes from their grandmother Yoeme. When Lecha abandons her son, Zeta takes him in and raises him as one of her own. Like Thelma in Ceremony Zeta grudgingly adheres to Indian rules of lineal descent which dictate that in the absence of her sister, the child becomes her responsibility. However despite ties to her Indian culture, Zeta makes her living in the modern world as a smuggler. Alongside the modern story of corruption, violence and revolution Silko has set the story of the almanac, its survival throughout history and its prophecies for the future of the human race. This again illustrates the duality of Silko's work which constantly combines the traditional and the contemporary.

Almanac also addresses the conflict of the rural and the urban landscape. As discussed previously, in Ceremony Silko locates the corruption of white society within an urban setting. In Almanac the city represents the influence of a white supremacist society and is the site of unrestrained violence and greed. Government officials who should be figures of law and order represent corruption and violence.

As St Clair states "The men charged with enforcing the law and upholding the principles of justice are among the most viciously criminal and egomaniacal characters in a novel full of egomaniacally lawless villains" (146) Perhaps the most extreme of these is Judge Arne, who presides over the federal district court in Phoenix. This man facilitates bribery and corruption in his court and his perversity knows no bounds. He is clearly hostile to women to the point that he must physically injure them during sex but his preferred sexual companions are his unfortunate basset hounds upon who he forces himself. The police chief of the city also represents a gross misuse of power. He runs a lucrative pornography business where he allows the torture and mutilation of suspects to be filmed. Corruption and violence have also infected the economic landscape of the novel. Trigg, a wheelchair bound businessman, deals in the acquisition and sale of human organs to West German biomedical companies. Trigg is possibly one of the most ludicrous characters in the novel. Paralysed from the waist down he claims to experience orgasms in his head due to his lack of ability to feel. However despite his absurdity, Trigg is one of Silko's most psychotic and dangerous individuals. His mission to find a cure for his paralysis leads him to murder countless hitchhikers and homeless men which he dismisses as being only "human debris. Human refuse" (444). He is careful to choose victims who are not "local or those with too many kin", Trigg believes he is improving and rehabilitating the urban landscape by getting rid of its undesirables- the blacks, Mexicans and homeless who crowd the streets. However he is further corrupting society in order to help himself. His actions, though illegal and immoral, are permitted and encouraged by a high court judge who signs court papers authorising everything. Another of Silko's corrupt characters, Beaufrey, has made his fortune smuggling and pushing drugs and also from the sale of torture pornography on the international market.

This man is another truly disturbing character, as his careless disregard for everyone around him renders him capable of horrendous acts-"the most bloody spectacles of torture did not upset him because he could not be seriously touched by the contortions and screams of imperfectly drawn cartoon victims" (533). Realising from a young age that "he had always loved himself, only himself" Beaufrey recognises the power this gives him over the people in his life (533). He uses drugs to enslave his boyfriend David as well as David's lovers Eric and Seese. The fact that his boyfriend has other lovers is irrelevant to Beaufrey until Seese becomes pregnant with David's child. Recognising that David could possibly grow to care for the baby, Beaufrey kidnaps and murders it, presenting David with photos of its mutilated corpse. When both Eric and David commit suicide, he makes a small fortune presenting pictures of their corpses as art. In contrast to Trigg, who is interested only in the economic value of his victims, Beaufrey regards his work as a game which he enjoys immensely. When he has "played" enough with David and Eric he calmly moves on to his next victim. The total indifference with which Beaufrey and Trigg regard killing represents the corruption which permeates every aspect of the urban setting in the novel.

In contrast to the greed and corruption which characterises the city and therefore modern society, the rural landscape of the novel represents a connection to the natural world which is associated with Indian culture. When Sterling, who grew up on an Indian reservation, remembers the years of the great depression he recalls that the Indians' reaction to it had been very different from that of the rest of America:

> It had made little or no impression on people at Laguna. Most, especially the old-timers, had said they never even knew a depression was going on, because in those days people had no money in banks to lose. Indians had never held legal title to any Indian reservation land, so there had never been property to mortgage. But winters those years had been mild and wet for the southwest. Harvests had been plentiful, and the game had been fat for the winter. The Laguna people had heard something about "The Crash". But they remembered "The Crash" as a year of bounty for the people (41).

In this case the Indians' connection to the natural world protected them from the disaster experienced by contemporary society. Just as the isolation of the rural landscape protected the Indians during the depression, so it also shelters Sterling and Seese from the violence of their lives. Seese is attempting to escape from a vicious cycle of drugs and violence created by Beaufrey, while Sterling is simply looking for a place of refuge after being banished by his tribe. Both these characters find a measure of protection and friendship working at the desert ranch which belongs to Zeta, one of the sisters charged with the protection of the almanac. However the rural setting in Almanac is different from that of Ceremony. It not only provides shelter, but also offers resistance to the corruption and immorality of the encroaching culture. Zeta's ranch in the desert is a home for Sterling and Seese but it is also the base of operations for her smuggling business. Unlike the smuggling associated with the city, which is symptomatic of a corrupt society, Zeta's business is depicted as a weapon of resistance against the white culture which is spreading like a disease. Both Zeta and her business partner Calabazas are using the white man's tools against him. They refuse to acknowledge the borders which were put in place by the white man and which represent the tyranny of his race. Calabazas argues that since his people's occupation of the land predates the white man's then their laws and geographical borders are illegitimate:

> We don't believe in boundaries. Borders. Nothing like that. We are here thousands of years before the first whites. We are here before maps or quit claims. We know where we belong on this earth. We have always moved freely. North-South, East-West. We pay no attention to what isn't real. Imaginary lines. Imaginary minutes and hours. Written law. We recognise none of that (216).

Zeta does not consider her business to be illegal because the white man's borders were formed on stolen land and so, according to her, are invalid:

> The people had been free to go traveling north and south for a thousand years, traveling as they pleased, then suddenly white priests had announced smuggling as a mortal sin because smuggling was stealing from the government. Zeta wondered if the priests who told the people smuggling was stealing had also told them how they were to feed themselves now that all the fertile land a along the rivers had been stolen by
> white men ... Stealing from the "Government"? ... How could one steal if the government itself was the worst thief. (133).

Both Zeta and Calabazas represent an interesting combination of the traditional and the contemporary. Although both characters have been influenced by the modern world, each of them has retained a vestige of his or her heritage. In her portrayal of these characters, Silko is once again demonstrating the dualistic tensions that inform her work.

In Almanac, Silko again reiterates the power of community in relation to the survival and wellbeing of the individual. Most of the characters in her novel illustrate the individualistic attributes of Western society which encourages the preservation of self over others. This challenges the traditional Indian belief that strength lies in belonging to a community.

Just as the white doctors in Ceremony encourage Tayo to think only of himself, so characters like Beaufrey and Trigg are completely self-serving. The landscape of Almanac is filled with beings whose only concern is for their own welfare. According to St Clair, "*Almanac* reveals an utterly amoral and atomised society in which each isolated member is indifferent to everything but the gratifications of his own enervated passions"(141). The character of Serlo is a perfect example of the individualistic notion of superiority represented by the wealthy. Descended from a line of aristocrats who raped Indian women because "they believed it was their God- given duty to "upgrade" mestizo and Indian

bloodstock", Serlo is in search of a race of pure blood white supremacists (541). Disgusted by any idea of contact with women, he saves and freezes his own semen in the hopes that one day he will father a race of superior human beings-"Investing his entire identity in his conviction of hereditary genetic superiority, he perhaps prefigures the end result of misogynistic, earth gutting, Eurocentric individualism" (St Clair 144). Convinced that the present human population has become genetically flawed and will eventually become extinct, Serlo invests vast amounts of money in Alternate Earth Modules which would be loaded with the last of earth's oxygen and launched into orbit around the earth. These modules would be a final refuge for a select few pure bloods who would "continue as they always had, gliding in luxury and ease across polished decks of steel and glass islands where they looked down on earth as they once had once gazed down at Rome or Mexico City from luxury penthouses, still sipping cocktails"(542). Serlo's connection to Beaufrey is based on their belief in the superiority of the aristocratic blood they share. Both believe that it is their god given right to rule over the masses because of their 'blue blood' or *sangre pura.* However as Sterling recalls, wealth and power in Tucson is intertwined with violence: "The Tucson mansions along mainstreet were the best proof that murderers of innocent Apache women and children had prospered. In only one generation government embezzlers, bootleggers, pimps, and murderers had become Tucson's "fine old families"" (80). Both Serlo and Beaufrey represent the individualistic notions of contemporary society. In contrast, characters from the minority groups are represented as a community which gains strength from sheer numbers. The twins leading the revolution, Tacho and El Feo, preach a message of inclusion, not exclusion. They invite all people to join their march if they are only willing to become part of a complete unit- "All were welcome. It was only necessary to walk with the people and let go of all the greed and the selfishness in one's heart. One must be able to let go of a great many comforts and all things European; but the reward would be peace and harmony with all living things"(710).
Both these leaders recognise that power is to be found in community and that by sheer strength of numbers the people can overcome the corrupt régime which rules Tucson.

The power and importance of community to the native peoples is examined in detail through the character of Sterling. Like Tayo, Sterling is a hybrid of Indian and white culture. Although he was born and raised on an Indian reservation Sterling spent most of his adult life working for the railroad and only returned to the reservation when he retired from his job. Because of this he is regarded as an outsider by his own people who mistrust his association with the white world. However neither is he fully accepted by contemporary society because of his ethnic identity. Sterling's expulsion from his tribe is as a result of his failure to prevent a camera crew from desecrating holy ground. He is given the job of protecting the tribe's sacred monuments because of his supposed knowledge of white culture. At his trial Sterling emphatically denies ever possessing such knowledge:"You act like I should have known everything just because I lived off the reservation. But I was working for the railroad. I was living in towns like Winslow or Barstow, not Hollywood ...I didn't have any experience of that sort of thing" (91). However these pleas fall on deaf ears and Sterling is banished by his tribe, condemned to live in the world he could not protect them from. Cast out by his people, he is seduced by many elements of contemporary society. Fascinated by the history of outlaws, he becomes a slave to the modern media, believing that everything he reads in white magazines is the truth. For most of the novel he stands on the periphery of two worlds- the traditional one from which he was expelled and a new society which horrifies him by its brutality. Like Tayo, Sterling's journey is cyclical and the novel ends with his return to the reservation and the reacceptance into his community. As a result Sterling exemplifies the importance of community and belonging to the native people. Characters without roots in the land often mistreat and are subsequently mistreated by the landscape itself.

Max Blue, a former New York mob boss, runs a successful assassination business from the luxurious surroundings of the golf course. His obsession with golf is symptomatic of his corruption, as this game represents the lifestyle of the rich which in Almanac is a symbol of a corrupt capitalist system. Convinced of his own invincibility Max refuses to vacate the course in the middle of a thunderstorm and is subsequently killed by lightening. Menardo, an Indian who rejects his heritage and embraces the materialistic concerns of western culture, is haunted by nightmares and becomes obsessed with protecting his own life to the point that he wears a bullet-proof vest day and night. Ironically it is this item that is responsible for his death as, convinced of its protective powers, he demands that his driver, Tacho, shoot him. However when Tacho stands too close the bullet pierces the vest and kills him. Leah Blue illustrates that corruption knows no gender boundaries when she manipulates the corrupt legal system into awarding her the underground water rights to an area of the Arizona desert in order to build a new Venice with elaborate water canals and fountains. Leah illustrates a shocking disregard for both the land she is destroying and the people whose lives she is affecting .Like Trigg, she works to secure the comfort of the rich at the expense of the poor. According to Jane Olmsted, "The extensive harm done to and by the many characters in *Almanac of the Dead* piles up evidence for the absolute necessity of recovery" (480).

Throughout the novel the possibility and then necessity of a revolution are presented. However Silko's revolution is not concerned with race. The uprising which ends the novel sees Indians, Blacks, Whites and Mexicans all marching together in complete harmony. Silko urges for a rejection of "all things European" which is a "condemnation of the dominant Euro-American disconnection among people, land and history that leads to dividing and exploiting the earth and its people for individualistic profit and gain" (Romero 626). Like Tayo in Ceremony, Silko believes her dual heritage qualifies her to speak for both the native and contemporary alike. According to her, the influence of European society has corrupted the Americas. The novel also illustrates Silko's view that, although traditions are crucial to the survival of the Indian culture, they must undergo a change in order to maintain their relevance. As such Almanac may be read as "an introduction to the next epoch of human history, a period to be intiated...by the disappearance of all things European"(Nelson 6).

Conclusion

Leslie Marmon Silko's work has enriched not only Native American Literature, but global literature since the 1970s. Her literary endeavors have called for "an upheaval in the world order and a dramatic revision of world history" (Sol 24).Critics such as Elizabeth Cook Lynn have praised novels like Almanac for its nationalistic approach to world events. However in later years some academics have condemned Silko for abandoning these nationalist concerns in order to gain the interest of mainstream readers. Her first novel Ceremony was a critical as well as a commercial success and was hailed as one of the most influential novels of its period. Almanac was also greeted with enthusiasm by the academic community which has praised its global scope and revolutionary message. Silko had spoken in several interviews about her wish to be considered as a global artist- "I see myself as a member of the global community. My folks who raised me saw themselves as citizens of the world. We see no borders. When I write, I am writing to the world, not to the United States alone" (Arnold 161). As a result of the novel's global scope Critics regard Almanac as an effort on Silko's behalf to engage an international audience. Her latest novel, Gardens in the Dunes, began as an attempt by the author to move away from the political scene and was initially intended to be an inoffensive tale tracing the ecology of the Americas - "I decided to write a novel about two women and their gardens and flowers. Absolutely no politics" (Arnold 161). However Silko soon discovered that even the ecology of the Americas is political- "But then I started to study the history of plants and where they came from… Right behind the conquistadors came the plant collectors…It turns out gardens are very political" (Arnold 161). Therefore, although the structure of the novel is traditional, the content is radically modern as Silko continues to examine the conflict which arises from the forced amalgamation of two diametrically opposed cultures.

In this book Silko returns to the binary structure which was so successful in Ceremony. Both the novel's form and content illustrate the author's dual sensibility as she continues to explore the motif of a native's separation from his/her people and eventual safe return. The novel is set in the 1900s at a time when the indigenous people of the Southwest and Mexican Northwest were driven from their homes to exile on federal reservations. The story follows a young Indian girl, Indigo, who is separated from her family when white settlers forcibly extricate the natives from their homes and relocate them on government reservations. Indigo is taken to a school run by whites so that she can be civilized and trained as a lady's maid. However, having run away from this school she is taken in by a wealthy plant collector, Edward, and his wife, Hattie. Hattie becomes taken with the child and so the couple decide to take her with them on their travels across America and Europe.

Gardens explores the conflict between the urban and rural, a theme previously examined by Silko in both Almanac and Ceremony. As before, Silko locates the corruption and greed of the modern world within an urban setting. The huge cities which Indigo encounters represent the wealth and glamour of the modern age. Magnificent parties, elaborate clothes and excessively rich food represent the decadence of European society. Shanty towns which sprang up as a result of the railroad and dam construction are also sites of prostitution, gambling and binge drinking. These towns are the source of the unrestrained corruption and violence which Silko associates with contemporary society. The rural setting of the novel provides the natives with a refuge from the brutality and degradation they suffer at the hands of the colonisers. In contrast to the inhabitants of the cities and shanty towns, who exhibit gluttony in every aspect of their lives, the native people of the novel live in a state of idyllic simplicity until they are invaded and forcibly removed from their homes.

In Gardens, Silko again presents the reader with the fatal collision between Indian and European cultures. However in this novel she chooses to examine the origins of this conflict and its immediate effects on the Indian people. In portraying the forceful abduction and re-education of Indian children, Silko is examining the very source of her own duality. Indian children were forced to remain at school for years at a time and were educated in the white way. By the time they returned to the reservations many of them were so alienated from the Indian way of life that they identified more with the Anglo society which had educated them than the traditions of their people. Like Tayo in Ceremony, Indigo is caught between the world of the traditional and the contemporary. She is forcefully taken from her simple life on the sand dunes and placed in the glamorous but destructive lifestyle of contemporary American and European society. Her Indian sensibilities constantly conflict with the modern attitudes she is expected to adopt. This is exemplified by her inability to adapt to using a bed, a prominent symbol of contemporary society. Indigo's connection with the natural world also confuses the white people around her. She makes friends with animals she meets and constantly gathers seeds of new plants she encounters in order that she may sow them for food when she returns to her homes in the sand dunes.

The character of Edward represents the destructiveness of contemporary society and so embodies the white witchery alluded to by Silko in her earlier work. He and his sister Susan participate in destructive forms of plant harvesting and relocation. Edward sees the natural world only in terms of its monetary value while Susan is interested only in the aesthetic aspect of plants and the social status which having rare specimens in her garden accord her. Both contrast sharply with Indigo and her people who live in harmony with the earth and understand the delicate balance of the natural world. Indigo is appalled when Edward takes her to see the removal of two giant beech trees, which Susan has decided would be an excellent addition to her garden- "Indigo was shocked at the sight: wrapped in canvas and big chains on the flat wagon was a great tree lying helpless, its leaves shocked limp, followed by its companion; the stain of damp earth like dark blood seeped through the canvas" (183). To Indigo the trees are living things which can feel pain at their destruction where Susan's only concern is that "the trees might not recover their vigor and appearance in time for the ball" (183). Edward and Susan's disapproval with Indigo throughout the novel reveal a deep seated desire for her subservience. Unable to accept that an Indian could consider herself the equal of white people, they constantly expresses a desire for her to conform to 'civilised' ways. Through her portrayal of these characters Silko seeks to remind her readers of the destruction that the colonisers wrought not only on the land but on the indigenous people of America.

In Gardens Silko uses the ecology of the Americas to represent the struggle between the world of the traditional and the contemporary. The plants of the novel are used as a symbol to represent the Indian people. Indigo, as the bridge between the two worlds, introduces new plants to the gardens which adapt to the new environment and thrive. Although she is awed by the wealth and glamour she observes in Italy, New England and England Indigo never loses her affinity for her own native traditions. Instead she uses her experiences in the modern world to her advantage when she returns to her home in the dunes. Through this character, Silko reiterates her view that the Indian people must adapt to changes occurring in their own culture and embrace these changes if they are to survive as a people. In an interview given in 1980, Silko revealed that she was interested in characters that "are survivors and [that] have a vitality to them. They might not have survived quite intact, but they survived" (Arnold 40). This is the quality which she herself exhibits and which many of her characters demonstrate.

The themes explored in all of her major novels to date illustrate Silko's unfailing belief in the need for change so that the Indian culture may survive and thrive in the modern world. By embracing her dual heritage, Silko has helped to reshape the field of contemporary American Literature. Her mixed blood status provides a bridge between the world of the traditional and contemporary, something which she exploits to great effect. Unlike other novelists such as N. Scott Momaday, who ends his novel House made of Dawn on a rather pessimistic note, the conclusions of Silko's novels are cautiously optimistic. Rather than dwelling on oppression, her works display a belief in the continuance and continuity of Natives cultures and values. She continues to explore the interfaces of Native American and Western worldviews with the traditional stories of her people used to great effect within a modern setting. Leslie Marmon Silko is a writer who understands perfectly her position at a cultural intersection and also the influence her work has on both traditional and contemporary communities. Her ability to respect the traditional while at the same time embracing the contemporary makes her one of the most important and influential writers of her generation.

Works Cited

Arnold, Ellen L, ed. Conversations with Leslie Marmon Silko. Jackson: University Press of Mississippi, 2000

Beidler, Peter G. Rev of Ceremony by Leslie Marmon Silko. American Indian Quarterly 3.4 (1997-1998): 357-358.

Brown, Alanna Kathleen. "Pulling Silko's Threads through Time: Am Exploration of Storytelling". American Indian Quarterly 19.2 (1995): 171-179.

Brown, Dee. Bury my Heart at Wounded Knee: An Indian History of the American West. London: Vintage, 1970.

Clements, William M. "Folk Historical Sense in Two American Authors". Native American Literature 12.1 (1985): 65-78.

Mitchell, Carol. "Ceremony as Ritual". American Indian Quarterly 5.1 (1979): 27-35.

Olmstead, Jane. "The Uses of Blood in Leslie Marmon Silko's "Almanac of the Dead"". Contemporary Literature 40.3 (1999): 464-490.

O' Meara, Bridget. "The Ecological Politics of Leslie Marmon Silko's Almanac of the Dead". Wicazo Sa Review 15.2 (2000): 63-73.

Page, Jake. In the Hands of the Great Spirit: The 20,000 Year History of American Indians. New York: Free Press, 2003.

Porter, Joy and Kenneth M. Roemer. The Cambridge Companion to Native American Literature. Cambridge: Cambridge University Press, 2005.

Romero, Chanette. "Envisioning a Network of Tribal Coalitions"". The American Indian Quarterly 26.4 (2002): 623-640.

Silko, Leslie Marmon. Ceremony. Harmondsworth: Penguin, 1986.

---. Gardens in the Dunes. New York: Simon & Schuster, 1999.

--- Almanac of the Dead. . New York: Penguin Books, 1991.

Sol, Adam. "The Story as its Told: Prodigious Revisions in Leslie Marmon Silko's "Almanac of the Dead"". American Indian Quarterly 23.3 (1999): 24-48.

St Clair, Janet. "Death of Love/ Love of Death: Leslie Marmon Silko's Almanac of the Dead". Melus 21.2 (1996): 141-156.

Swan, Edith. "Feminine Perspectives at Laguna Pueblo: Silko's Ceremony". Tulsa Studies in Women's

Literature 11.2 (1992): 309-328.

Weaver, Jace. "Native American Authors and Their Communities". Wicazo Sa Review 12.1 (1997): 47-87.

Works Consulted

Barnett, Louise & James Thorson, Eds. Leslie Marmon Silko: A Collection of Critical Essays. Albuquerque: University of New Mexico Press, 1999.

Bell, Virginia. "Counter Chronicling and Alternative Mapping in Memoria del Fuego and Amlanac of The Dead". Melus 25.3 (2000) 5-30.

Bird, Gloria. "Towards a Decolonisation of the Mind and Text: Leslie Marmon Silko's *Ceremony*". Wicazo Sa Review 9.2 (1993): 1-8.

Brown, Dee. The American West. London: Pocket Books, 1994.

Chavkin, Allan, ed. Leslie Marmon Silko's Ceremony: A Casebook. Oxford: Oxford University Press, 2002.

Cook Lynn, Elizabeth. "The American Indian Fiction Writer: 'Cosmopolitanism, the Third World, and First Nation Sovereignty'". Wicazo Sa Review 9.2 (1993) : 26-36.

Curtis, Edward S. The North American Indian. London: Taschen, 2005.

Piper, Karen. "Police Zones; Territory and Identity in Leslie Marmon Silko's *Ceremony*". American Indian Quarterly 21.3 (1997): 483-497.

Roemer, Kenneth. "Contemporary American Indian Literature: The centrality of Canons on the

Margins". American Literary History 6.3 (1994): 583-599.

Silko, Leslie Marmon. Storyteller. New York: Arcade Publishing, 1981.

Swan, Edith. "Healing via the Sunwise Cycle in Silko's *Ceremony*". American Indian Quarterly 12.4

Wood, Karenne. Rev of Gardens in the Dunes by Leslie Marmon Silko. American Indian Quarterly 23.2 (1999): 71-72.

Acknowledgements

I would like to thank my supervisor Dr Lee Jenkins for her continued help and support throughout the year. I am also grateful to Dr Padraig Kirwan of the University of London, whose enthusiasm for the subject was a constant motivation. I would like to thank my family and my friends who are my reason for living and for laughing. Anne, thanks for all the motivating phone calls and Gill, thanks for the laughter, the stress and most importantly, the Java.